A HOUSE OF BRANCHES

A House of Branches

Poems by

Janisse Ray

WIND PUBLICATIONS

International Standard Book Number
    Hardcover 978-1-936138-21-0
    Softcover 978-1-936138-14-2

Library of Congress Control Number 2010925962

First edition

Cover design — Eleonora Alcalde Machado
Front cover art — "Piedmont Savanna" by Philip Juras

For Rick Bass

Table of Contents

II.

III

I

Kingfisher

The sidewalk was crowded
the evening the kingfisher fell.
People stopped, staring
at the ground, then up.
It just dropped from the sky,
a woman said.
Above,
Chittenden Bank rose
shining, four stories high.
Windows were dusky sky,
the river meters away.

Kingfishers: I know their chants
by heart. I've watched
hundreds dive,
rise,
fly off.

But once I held
a kingfisher
in my hands,
I touched its blue power.
That may be the only time
I ever do.

What I held was more precious
than handfuls of money.
If I could have restored it
to wind, I would have.

What to do
with the wild pain?
was the question,

and the answer —
carry it
across Elliot Street
to the bushes by the church,
to the flowers,
and set it down.
Slip it inside
an envelope of green.
Give it back.

Give it back, all
of it, and go home.

Edge of the World

In the dead tree by the brackish pond,
in pouring rain, four great egrets

preoccupy the somber sky
with its gray burden of rain,

a native orchestra playing
outstretched boughs of cedar,

notes ringing down stalks of spartina,
pattering into the pond.

Shrimp and minnows rise
in circles that quickly go silent.

What can I say I have
accomplished in this life?

Can I say I stood in solidarity with rain
as it stormed a bilging marsh,

or that I remained loyal to egrets
on gray reaches of cedar?

Can I say my allegiance
rested strong with cordgrass?

Have I stayed true to the great blue heron
balanced on one wand of leg,

evenings, in the same dead tree;
faithful to the fiddler crab;

and to the wood stork
with its hindrance of bill at ebb tide?

Can I say I never abandoned them
but was violent in fidelity?

Moon over Maryland

I had been traveling all day north along the interstate, city after
city. I had seen a tower in South Carolina made like a sombrero —
people climbed into the crown. A monument to cigarettes in
Virginia rose one hundred feet tall. Somewhere in Delaware a
couple dozen grown trees had been wrapped with light, their limbs
lit glass. In a tunnel a mile long beneath Washington Bay I went
underwater and breathed. All day I had seen highways on top of
highways, concrete arches through space,   pavement as far
as the future could see.

So that when a lopsided ball of orange light lifted from the
hazy fringe of trees in what the signs said was Maryland, I
thought it another human construction — an almost perfect
rendition but too orange, flattened at the top — and it would
not take long hurling at seventy miles an hour to reach
          this new attraction.

As I drove the orb faded. As I drove it lifted, until finally above the
glittering lights of endless city it hung too high for human feat.

I have come to love the moon. I have learned its habits. It is the
only moon we will ever have. Nothing will be able to take it away.

Questions to a Grasshopper

Grasshopper, do you have a husband
waiting for you at home, under some sumac
roof? Or a son who yet needs you?
In the grasshopper bank, is your account
low? Is the *Times* waiting on an article
that you must squeak up out of your armored
head and from what you have deciphered
with those waving wands?
Is the rent due on your leaf, and do you
have to pay somebody for the water that falls free
from the sky? To whom do you owe your food?
Are you paying for grasshopper roads and
grasshopper schools and grasshopper hospitals
and grasshopper police and some kind of insect
library filled with wondrous leafy scrolls?
Do you have a president? Are you asked
to fight, to kill your own? Must you pay for it?
Or are you free, as you seem, to go
bursting through stalks of dry grasses,
among strawberry leaves and yarrow,
curious and flippant, without direction,
unwary, obligated to nothing?

Bird-Banding with the Biologists

Rufous-sided towhee,
when I hold you, you are mine,
and when I release, you pause unblinking
before you take to wings not one of us has.
I love that.

White-throated sparrow, Carolina wren,
must I capture you to know you?
and how lucky I am this dawn
to walk the mist net, a human spider web
appearing and disappearing in the weak fog.

The sun yawns and stretches.

Oh cardinal, you take my breath
as I draw you from the cotton bag,
careful of your sharp beak.
You are the color of spilled blood,
an oak fire's embers.
No human has feathers red enough for me.

The man from Antarctica tells me of
living in a tent in ice with a year's
supply of food, cans and cans, Shakespeare
to read in the unbroken white silence.
The penguins are there.
The bottom of their colony, he says,
is hotter than hell.
It will disintegrate tin cans.

He comes back, tied with bags,
a bird hunter. We record
their weight, sex, body fat,

give them their registry number
on a tiny silver bracelet they wear
around wishbone legs.

Then, for a moment,
we see them for what they are:
birds in hand, creatures of air,
songboxes of spring mornings
migrating across landscapes
of our design
and we praise them:

Oh kinglet, Oh oriole,
tell us what you know.

Field Guide for Wildlife Clinics

The goshawks in their cages
do not wish to hear recordings
of the boreal forest, a particular
longing of wind in aspens, calls
of saw-whet owls and the skitter
of red-backed voles in leaves.

Nor do broken-winged warblers
in wicker baskets desire the
piped music of eastern deciduous
slopes in late spring, exaltations
of redstarts and thrushes, cranes
like sky-flowers, honking.

Nor record for the swallow-tailed kite
staring with one good eye
the relief of waves lapping a beach
after migration, purl of dolphin, yaw
of curlew and boat-tailed grackle,
wind arranging black needlerush.

There is no returning.
Better to play Nina Simone,
oh children, go where I send you.
Or Van Morison, Etta Mae Baker.
In your own room, broadcast
swamp-moans while you sleep.

Eleventh

I know where
the ribbon snake
lives—
under the maple
by the barn.
One day when I
was there
a dead leaf
crackled like fire
and I saw her,
slip of green
I followed
around the waist
of the tree,
through already
dying grass.
When she turned
to face me, eyes
burning, she
studied me.
I — wanting
to feel her softness,
her certainty, the stove
of her tiny heart —
touched one finger,
only one,
upon her perfect tail.
At that moment
the tree opened
and she wound
inside, her
passageway
dark and narrow.

Long before
I turned away,
no doubt,
she lay
on her mat of earth
at the bottom
of the maple,
among the roots,
strip
of brilliant
kindling.
The eleventh
commandment is
love the earth,
love the tree,
love the snake.

Riding Bareback through the Universe

The earth does not move steadily,
spinning at one speed through the heavens,
but with the motion
of a wild stallion at full gallop
across a painted desert,
which is sweep and fall, sweep and fall.
The earth is waltzing.
Its cloud-tail streams behind like a comet's.
Not only the earth. Every heavenly body
once thought steady, plodding even,
flings itself along with senseless joy.
In the sky an ecstasy of stars
stampedes through the universe.
You and I ride standing
on the back of earth,
feet firmly planted, side by side,
our love for this life
so thunderous and billowing,
so wild and powerful,
we finally understand celestial motion.
Around us thousands of leaves
leap up and down on their stems
and summer flowerheads
surge with the wind.

Noticing

1.

I would not have seen the web
a spider strung between us and sky
except the sun crested the cliff
along the Bay of Fundy. Finally
our long night beside Mill Creek
was over: I greeted the light.
A shimmer is not a moon-blade,
not the disk of sun plating
tips of red spruce silver.
So much depends on where one looks —
upward! — and when. So much
is happenstance, accident, grace.
Too often the little voices
that say "See!" and "There!" are silent.

2.

But I see the web,
nothing more than
another life, noticed,
which is our job
while we are here.

3.

Notice how quickly the bay
recedes, abandoning more
of its red-pebbled beach,

leaving rocks blanketed
with orange seaweed.
Notice how, back along the cliff,
white asters with gold disks
bloom in pockets
of loose mineral, and the
strange branched milkweed
hangs with frittalaries.

Rescue

(one of the stories the game wardens told)

A swamp is not a cathedral, with its downed logs,
sponge of floor, the greens and browns
dovetailing, though the sky is fairest blue

through hump-drawn cypress.
There are places to say what's too big
to be said in smaller places.

But in a swamp you go round in circles.
A swamp has only one side, the way *out* the
way *in*. A river has a mouth.

What drove the man here, tearing open
fog with his outboard? What had gone so
wrong? If he had done this on the street,

suddenly yelling at sky above
buildings, going down on his knees
at the curb, he would be in a madhouse.

The officers said when they found him,
he was hollering loudly,
as I too have stood arms upstretched,

close to death as only in dying are we truly
of God. Every ounce of flesh desperate.
The breath coming in chunks only

God can gather in his big, invisible
hands and recreate. *Make me worthy of my life,*
O God, and my life worthy of me.

17

In the swamp I am certain without a doubt
God has been there, is there.
The man was certain, I'm sure he was, that

God listened from spaces between molecules —
the staining amid green ceremonies
of bay leaves, along rivulets of dark

gullies of bark, in the seeping water itself
that turns the blue reflection of God.
God heard what he had to say. What I wonder

is, did God answer? Did he move toward the man
through the trees? If the man loved this life
he would be glad the officers came,

for if God had reached him first,
wading high ground from the Great Beyond,
robe gathered out of water's reach,

the man never would have been found.

Service

To the quiet woods
every Sunday morning
a man comes. I have seen him,
although more often I note
his bicycle at the opening
of the path

leading to a pond.
Through trillium,
jewelweed and cranesbill,
Jack in the pulpit. Fir. Fallen
feathers of ravens and owls.
Mossy maple polypore.

At the spring the man
faces cold water, west,
then delivers three long cries,
not animal, not human.
I hear him ululate.
I know him by the morning.

I have not seen what other
ceremonies he makes.
Except one morning
when fog pitched the hill-
pasture, where the sun
first arrives, I watched

the man stand with his face
to that brimming fire,
white light washing over him,
firmament and temples
ablaze. He raised his arms and
beat his chest with his fists.

Creation Story

Across the backbone of barrier spit
toward Goose Island although not that far.

Through articulate and wizened arms
of live oak that gather
the lyrics of red-winged blackbirds

and cravings of towhees. Past raceme
of coral bean. Into black needlerush

strung with dew, thigh-cold
and thick.

Toward belly of bay flash,
tang of mullet,
ruddy ground dove's whir-burst,
marsh wren sunk from sight.

In the skittish crown of cabbage palm

a great blue heron has constructed
her driftwood nest

stick upon stick.

She guards it hunch-necked,
growling, yellow bill agape,
fierce

in her charge.

Cardinal Flowers

The pope himself would bless them,
how they keep the faith, standing
council along the Wakulla
mid-September, as usual, in crested
cassocks of a scarlet so pious:
Surely it is the blood of the master.
At vespers we float past them,
praying to see, as they do,
ruby-throated hummingbirds
fanning at their robes.

All Art Has Three Subjects

In the savanna bog, where rainfall moves
in slow running sheets, pinewoods tree frog
crouches above a water column
inside the mouth of pitcher plant *flava*,
awaiting the fly that invariably surrenders to sweet.

The tree frog feeds, then defecates
a rising mound, body parts of insects
sodden with nitrogen. That dark milk,
in turn, drains to the heart of the red-stalked
carnivore. It blossoms brilliant yellow.

From here life ebbs, from here it springs
without question — life and death, death and life.
Yet one cannot help but think of love.
The flower loves the sky that loves the bog
that loves how the fly loves even the frog.

Fire-Wings I

Can the fire of monarchs be blown out,
millions of orange candles extinguished
by wild snow and wind racing
across the Mexican sierra?

Just like that, in one cold breath,
could all the monarchs be gone?

A butterfly's body is nothing
but a notch of hollow reed
glued to scraps of paper wings.
Ardent and flammable,
it was not made to last.

One by one monarchs stiffen
and drop from their gray masses
to the forest floor, wings clamped, undressing
the firs to the unexpected winter night.

The bigger question is, What
would the world be like
without monarch's incandescence,

without the knowledge scripted
in the slender volumes of its wings?

Who would ring the bells of spring
and bells of fall in the bell-towers
along migration routes?

Who would deliver messages of wildflowers,
converse with ditch weeds,
and croon over stalks of milkweed
cradling rows of pearly eggs?

And what, in a world without
monarchs, would set
human yearning aflame?

Tympanum

At night a wind sweeps low over salt marshes
south of Highway 98, addressing the ocean.
For thousands of miles the wind has come,
from the Arctic Circle across the backbone

of the Appalachian Chain, unbraided by zones
of trees, roiled by liaisons of atmosphere and terrain.
Stirred by puny wings, rent by sun,
it has collected the good humor of land.

It has been breathed, exhaled, and comes
to meet Gulf winds full of life it has known.
Its history palpable. The wind journeys to the bottom
of the continent to play in one sabal palm

fanning a dike. If there has been no rain all day,
the palm is dry. Its fronds, tipped by tiny
brass tongues, sing in the language of scorpions.
Strings and reeds fill the great hall.

On the Beach One Summer Night
After Hearing the Algae Is On

The road along the dunes is broken like a bottle,
dashed by hurricane. Under a keel of moon
we maneuver its shoal of sharp asphalt

toward the darkness of the ocean, reminded
that our faults harden useless and ugly,
like old glue. Tide out, we cross salt flats

to enter finally an electric current.
Around us, the Gulf is charged, storm of weeds,
phytoplankton's riot, water on fire. Around us

mullet dart and flop, comets in bioluminescence,
neon trails through India ink. Splash, glitter, flare.
Dripping, our clothes kindle.

Everything we do makes a mark.
But in stillness we undo, in stillness extinguish
the glowing wakes of Lucifer's bloom.

Be still, then.
Very still.

Moon-Set at St. Marks

bright sickle used
by the bent farmer of the salt
marsh slowly sinks

into mud flats as he
shuffles home with his heavy
sack of crabs

Hunting Deer

At night a race of deer press hoof
prints into the sandhills.

The deer pause beneath this very laurel oak.
Ghost-buck paws the ground,

scrapes bark from saplings.
He chews a moment on a twig.

All afternoon above evidence of them I wait

still as an acorn or scrap of lichen,
rifle on knees.

She who has been one of us, they will say
tonight

in velvet voices, then throw back their heads
and laugh.

Across the Wilderness

The first night we camp
in an apron of meadow.
The fire is orange,
its flames small as needles.
It pierces water clean,
West Fork of the Sun,
too high to cross.
A brace of deer
frame a far pine as I come
over a swale. Stepping back,
I crouch in brindled grass
to watch their vigil.
Hours later they haven't moved.
We have all been in meadows
where deer turn to rock
amid lupines, mirth
of wildflowers whose bones
we wish we knew.
Bear scat by the river is real.
Why does the wind laugh?
In the night the meadow
tells the grizzly
and the mountain lion
where we are.
By mid-morning
we cut ourselves loose.
We lob fire-blackened rocks
into the creek, scatter
our ashes, more to appease
than anything.

Knowing wilderness
can change its mind.
When we resume
the paintbrush trail, the wind
is too familiar with our faces.

The Fall of Civilization

Today I'll be antelope.
I'll run along the riverbank,
through cottonwood and willow,
wind between my teeth.
I'll stand with one foreleg
lifted, sniff all directions.
I'll bolt until I come
to a free meadow.
I'll taste any fruit at all.
If it rains I'll be in it.

The violet-green swallow will take my place.
She'll perch in the hard chair and worry
about papers on the floor. She'll flutter
over and peck at them, pull one out
with her beak. Then another. Drop them.
She'll circle and straighten each pile.
Then she'll fly to the window to watch other
swallows happening by. For a long time
she'll sit on the sill, and when she turns away
a strange look will bewilder her face.
Pausing at the mirror, she'll preen:
emerald coverts, purple quiver of
primaries, each ivory-stalked rachis.
Vanes to catch wind just so. The calamus
with its purpose. She'll try not to watch the clock.
She will pick up a book and think

on a sunny day when the wind is right...

II

Bone Deposit

When I am dead, put my bones in Georgia
that made them. Give her back the calcium,
phosphorous, the holy manganese that serve
me well, keepers of this unruly flesh.
When I am dead, let me honor land
that struck fire and offered to hungry air
a skeleton pieced of earth that holds
my spirit upright in the spinning and spiraling
of this world. The bones claim me, until I
return time and again to her soil, trapped,
wondering what I search for, what calls me back,
why a body is never free. Ossein of story,
marrow's elements — that debt will be paid.

What Happened to Georgia

for Steve Wright

Big Sandy Creek where you learned to swim
bilges muddy, lapping up orange pigment
of eroding flatwoods, cut and turned.
The white watery eyes of kaolin mines
stare up out of Wilkinson County.
Some evil presses a razor into their hands
and kneeling over Georgia — all her beauty —
they take her down. Oh Georgia.

When the blade is dull they rinse and scrape.
All day you and I have asked each other, *Why?*
from the porch swing of Uncle Avys's cabin,
What happened to Georgia? What of our people?
We are the ones she calls home.

At dusk we take bourbon to the dock
where willow hangs and bottlebush blooms.
A rainbow emerges from drizzling clouds.
The arc repeats in the lake, until a perfect
hoop of ribbons, its colors bright and vivid,
holds us holy in the iris of its fleeting eye,
its marriage of love and squander.

Slave Canal

Thanks to the slaves who dug this canal,

halfway down the Wacissa, mouth
hidden in willow — long gash that runs
straight to the Aucilla, aiming
cotton to sea. Its water is deep
black.

We run it.

The dead, hundreds strong, row us
forward. Limestones
wide and thick as men's torsos
line the banks, so the tragedy
preserves itself, as it will.

The water lilts in sorrow that cannot be
washed away, nor undone.

We see the Florida they saw.

Sabal palms shake with wind. Then high hush.
Alligators flail, worry us. Plops of turtles
and frogs, portent of secrets.
White-tailed deer come to drink.
Water moccasin. Red maple. Magnolia.
Bog frogs sound perpetual evening.

This is not a tribute
for the fidelity of their deaths,
for terrible love and impossible labor.
This is our thanks.

Because the earth has accepted that long scar.
Because the water has pardoned its division.
Because we have not forgotten.

Boat Ride at Wakulla Springs

By lying about the fare and hustling them
past the ticket counter, we hoodwinked
our parents onto a flat-bottomed boat
that circles the Wakulla River.

They preferred a flea market, they said,
where you can take something home, until
the river wrapped its arms around them
like sleepy children. Disappearing sun

struck wide across the swamp, alligators
on high tussocks. Moorhens with scarlet
beaks scuttled among swaying grasses,
unchaining great pearls of apple snails.

Our father, on and off his feet, praised
the deer, anhingas with wings outspread,
water snake draped through wild roses,
gray log knotted with seven Suwannee cooters.

Wood ducks parted the blue pickerel-weed.
Turkey vultures, readying for night,
lowered by the dozens in easy loops, knitting
a black curtain slowly through the cypress.

When the ride ended
we walked off the boat empty-handed.

Okefenokee Swamp

In this sweetwater wash, copper shafts of snakes
develop among cypress. Boles upstretch

to green bodices, the wrinkled circles of knees.
Thigh-like buttresses settle a trembling earth.

If it weren't for cypress the dark
water would dive forever.

Prothonatary warblers like small suns orbit
sweet bay magnolia with its white-threaded leaves

and the shed tongues of loblolly bay. Obsidian
channels penetrate the titi, shackled to the swamp's

emerald heart. Turtles are fluent in the act
of immersion. The sawgrass prairie is crisscrossed with wakes.

At its edge a great egret, stark
white and spindly, a black-stemmed flower,

curls into the landscape, wings outspread.
I close my eyes into its image, etched on the plates

of my lids, corrosion of landscape centuries old.
I am not afraid to die.

Virgin Cypress

In memory of Carolyn Hodges,
guide to old-growth cypress
on Lewis Island, in the Altamaha delta

She is the one who first took me. Although the tide was going
out there was enough water. Mullet were jumping. Lightning
flashed between smoldering clouds, and an osprey
followed us up Rifle Cut.

There is more to this world than can be seen: black current
beneath, pulling this way, then that. She did not say much more
than *mouth*, than *start*, and pointed. *Tie the boat here, follow*
the orange ribbons hanging from the brush. Most of the time
there is no path.

The trees were so old they were ethereal, and between them
flag iris rose like blue throats whose silence is a ceremony of
mud. I knew finally why dead wood glows.
It rises and burns.

Such a short time we have, with the grace of moon, to navigate
the narrow places, until we come to the river. Which knows as
much of us as we of it. Which shows no mercy. Which repeats
our names as it drains the marshes. In a litany of moans the
oysters let go their last swallows.

Now my friend is foxfire, bright flame roving through the
delta, luminous copper ball at night rising along the Altamaha,
on Butler and on Lewis, as a tumult of frogs fills the darkness,
over and over crying *Hallelujah*.

The Resuscitation

On a shank of highway that rends
the national forest, where oaks shed
mast into palmetto hammocks and
wild boars root in the wilderness,

a shape cast of night stepped into
a funnel of high-beams. A woman swerved,
braked hard, saw as it crumpled
a black bear. A thousand hairstreaks

lifted toward her throat.
The world tipped, spilling a legion
of stars. She raked through them
toward the bear.

Its jacket, familiar as a lover's,
trailed on the shocked pavement.
The soft insides of her forearms
ached. *Breath!* she thought, went

for the heart, same side, felt a bird
fluttering in her hands.
Closed its muzzle, mouth on snout
breathed in, tasting on her tongue

bark of titi, hint of berry, out
and in again, out and in, out. No matter.
The bear moaned in final ululation.
The bear's last call

swept the dark, rank swamp,
sliding across roots of cypress,

black tupelo, past cross vine clinging
to planer tree, trembling ghost

webs of spider lilies lifting from
mouldy silt, passing across
arched backs of chorus frogs and
yellow-crowned night herons,

washing through skimpy nests, each
woven of twenty-nine sticks
in the egret rookery, filling the long
finger of black racer's track.

The bear was more than in life
untouchable. At its shoulder
pennywort knotted in ragged umbels.
The woman lay down beside it and waited.

Nocturne

Sometimes when barred owls are courting
in the south woods, hooting and hollering
far into the night — they who have no hands
to hold their love, who have only songs
and the big brown moons of their eyes
that see in the dark — sometimes I dream
I am one of them. You are the other.

Noiseless you land on a poplar branch
whose leaves have fallen like feathers.
Desire is a white-tailed rabbit,
talon-limp and silky. Its hot blood
will not be wasted. You cry black water.
I cry moonlight. If there is a god of owls
we have her permission.

Take me as I am, you sing to all
who listen in the night. *My queen,*
for the love of rabbit, for the love of love,
fly with me into the ravine. Come
singing the night's deep love-call.
Flower of moon, silent-eyed ravener, fly.

Through open windows of the houses
men and women of the fields are stirring
in their beds, turning and reaching out
hands like sleepwalkers crossing
pastures and entering old trees.
We glide through silver air beyond,
to a deeper place I dream.

Site Fidelity

Bright with history, birds
nest in the syrup shelter,

wood shed, coral honeysuckle
winding the gray fence.

Nuthatch enters the oak that
spilled last summer's storm.

I am torn between saving
the corn crib, with its powdery logs,

or starting anew,
wrens in a coffee can.

Pileated, your red the spark
of my grandmother, tell me

what the place was like, back
then, before the world began?

Towhee, whose wings fan each
day aflame: tell me what

has been forgotten.
We think history ends

when elders die: ask Wood-
pecker to hush her laughing.

I am the middle daughter
of my grandfather's absence.

Nothing belongs to us.
I try to keep what I can,

flint points my uncles brought
from the fields, among globes

of resin in a rusty tin. Tell me,
Kestrel, how they got here.

Swallow-tailed Kite, you who keep
account of the generations,

pass to me their lost stories,
the sun and the forest,

babbling creek, all ghosts
and nothing born to last.

Drouth

For six weeks without rain
the crops were irrigated with water
from a pond formed by a dam
across an unnamed creek that
drained a thousand acres of the farm.

In six weeks the pond fell eight feet.
What was hidden was brought to light:
curvature of bank, black bases
of trees. Bluestem germinated
where it would never grow.

In Fitzgerald, rain doused flower
gardens, and even in Osierfield,
half mile away, wet one side of the road
where the farm did not lay, left
the other as dry as yearning.

One morning, crossing the dam,
I counted a few great egrets
among fifty wood storks,
fishing the drying shallows.
A wood stork will travel

a hundred miles to feed,
because they don't stalk or dive.
They blunder. They live by chance,
of touching with probing bill
minnow, crayfish, shiner.

A wood stork's life is one long risk.
That summer we waited for rain
under inscrutable skies. Corn and

soybeans withered in the fields.
All we could count on

were wood storks flowering
in the shrinking ponds, how the pliers
of their upturned beaks gnawed
at the sky, fish glinting like coins.
In many ways they were payment.

Naming the Unseen

for Milton Hopkins

I.

The man who devoted his life to birds
can no longer hear them sing:

> high-frequency warblers
> trilling through rib-cages of
> trees, screech owls
> moaning over threads
> of evening, lost notes of
> sparrows.

He sees. When we walk the lane
toward the dam, watching for sandhill cranes
that scratch their dances
in the fields, for Mississippi kites
to rise on thermals, watching
the way the brief light creeps across the farm
he says:

> blue grosbeak
> rough-winged swallow
> hairy woodpecker
> indigo bunting.

One morning a hawk broke from the hardwood
drain across the young pines.

> *Broad-winged*, he said. It shrieked,
> high. *Can you hear it?* I asked.

I miss that, he said.

Along Little Ocmulgee he keeps asking
if the Acadian flycatcher is calling.
It goes like this.

    Chee-unk, cheee-unk.

A brown-headed nuthatch sputters
by — just one, curious. Above, where
the river parts the sky, a buzzard
lavishly swirls.

II.

Imagine if the woods were silent as a photograph.
Imagine if the ears of trees recalled nothing.
Imagine that what is there finally isn't.

The tupelo piles rosy fingers on the swamp floor.
Decomposing, they part the black leaves.
Their memory is shaken air, a long offering to the sun.

The silence leaves them dumb.

Psychoanalysis

What does it mean, Sigmund Freud,
that the snake was not in my dream
but in the hallway, a brown velvet rope
stretched across the runner. It glimmered
like an Indonesian textile, new-
woven, lying across the path we travel
dozens of times a day between kitchen
and bedroom, front and back.
I called my husband, who
came from the porch and stood
opposite, length of perfect cord
between us. Strange as it was,
we were stranger. We watched,
only that, never moving
for broom or bag, no impediment.
We watched it glide across the floor,
behind a row of machines, hot water
heater, washer and dryer, through
a drift of spilled laundry powder, into
the accumulation of our lives, old
rag bag, dog shampoo, shoe polish,
spot remover, brushes and brooms,
window cleaner, jugs of vinegar,
ammonia and bleach.
Our lives are no place for you, beautiful,
this house no crevice in an old tree.
For your own sake, get out.

Spawn

Cleaning the fish
underneath the pear tree
among white blossoms
shaken from the tree
leaves shad scales
among the petals.

Orchard

Across the field overgrown with wild asters, persimmons hang
as they have each fall, translucent coral. Soon first frost will
turn autumn hoary. Then in the silver field the persimmon tree,
rationing fruit, will fool deer with its wide, flame-colored leaves.

At dusk we sift pears from the sky. If the sun threw more gold
we could not breathe. I am the tree, thrashing. Pears in a meteor
shower thud against thick, uncombed grass, tight to warm
earth. A barred owl answers from the woods.

We are still here. We are happier than ever.

The Design of Autumn

Any day the hawks, circling
overhead, will be gone. Perhaps today
their last. The trees throw off

bushels of paper money, collecting
in the weeds. The leaves are loud
when the wind comes off the hill.

Who can lie down at the time of
ripe fruit, of decadence, before
blackness? No matter how rich

we become, or old, or unable,
won't some part of us desire to weave
a basket in which to forage

the last of the grapes? Or, start
moving toward the valleys of deer?
I go wandering greedily

amid all the falling-down.

On Traveling

An evening after hard work all day,
       my love wanted to walk through the pasture
           past the bog,
               looking.

Pitcher plants were blooming!
       In a scrubby copse, a calf lay
           in leaf-creche, being licked
               alive.

Dewberries among thorny vines
       were darker than dusk, and sweet.
           When we stepped into the pasture
               the dog

chased the herd of cows. They
       stampeded this way then that
           like a cloak of cedar waxwings.
               Behind

the watering hole, the woods open
       to a bottomless head, a creek, quicksand.
           My father once plunged a cane pole
               twenty feet.

I never go in but stand under water oaks
       listening to bullfrogs.
           This evening was no different,
               except

hundreds of tiny meteors were spinning
       through red maple and tulip poplar,
           lighting, burning out,
               re-lighting.

Fireflies!
       like I hadn't seen since girlhood,
            each carrying a tiny lantern,
               searching

high and low for beloveds who waited in the trees
       without announcement. Any other place
           we might not have seen them,
              any other night.

The secret gathering-place of fireflies is found.
       We have at last arrived on the far side
           of the world, as far as is possible
             to go.

Land of Milk and Honey
(An Homage)

1. *milk*

the moon a pond of magnolia
petals. porcelain moonflowers
twining bleached bones
of deer. china saucers scraping
the whitewashed cupboard.
enamel pan. white-hot water singing
against the lacy skull of milch cow.
milkweed fluff tugged from its pod
by seven white horses of wind. breasts
beneath cotton gowns of ibis-winged
women. panting of the women.
cirrus throats of sparrows.
panther claw scratching
at a parchment window. moth papers.
hairs of my grandmother
cupping white eggs of doves.
powdery ashes of white oak, sifted
through the moon's cheesecloth.
fog of the morning of every
twig's birth and winter child's
breath tatting tiny flowers.
dew on gardenias like buttermilk.
meringue on a frothy creek.
tablecloth clattering its teeth.
the evening star hissing through
faded arms of white sycamore.

2. *honey*

slant of October sun on tupelo
hives. saddlebags of worker bees
spilling gunpowder to Sunday.
drone of barred owls.
catacombs of fertile eggs
from rusty chickens. iron bolts.
wagon tongues groaning
with the weight of coming night.
feathers of crowing cocks.
tannic Ten Mile Creek pouring
toward the golden river, morning
of the river. humps of cypress.
poplar hand-hewn into table,
axe-handle and bowl. sumac.
the hawk's red tail dripping
gallberry. wildflower fire
inside a brick chimney above
a thousand chipping sparrows.
thunder-showers of longleaf burrs,
early fall on red clay.
rainwater funneling toward
the branch, past stone crockery
filled with brown eggs.
outside the window, dun fields
of clover, millet, sorghum.
warm bread and an open jar.

Reply to a Letter

Those bushy trees are willows.
Not weeping but black.
Between them river birch.
Lots of hawthorne.
Back in the swamp — tupelos,
swamp chestnut oak, red maple.
You are lucky to have Miriam.
Because she loves birds she loves beauty
and to desire the hidden habits
of warblers is to desire another world,
one of mystery, to know
how things come to us and where they go.
I'm glad you have taken her
into the oxbow lakes and cut the motor.
Parulas are there, in rusty willows.
Hoodeds and yellow-throateds.
Bright prothonataries among
brown tangles of swamp.
It's something to see.
Something to hang on to.
Those dead lakes where you took Miriam
when you were a young married couple
so long ago —
most people never see that world,
though they are in it and beside it
always, as you say.
Think of your heroic fortune.
Think of blindness.
There is still time to learn all the words
the swamp calls itself — pignut
hickory, buckeye, overcup oak.
This planet should be called Serendipity.
We would name the willows
Holy Holy.

III

Revolution

Sometimes when I am lost in the rolling gray sadness
of cities,

sometimes driving in my automobile

on the wide dead rivers of interstate highways

I see a meadow, burnished grass, pond
like a medallion, grape
arbor twining small green hands.

I see myself go to the great white switch
that keeps the refrigerator running and the saw
spinning and the light connecting its circuitry,
that keeps factories pumping, drillers
whetting appetites, dozers and treecutters
grinding and growling and grating and greasing,
that doesn't neglect the gun-makers.

In one galvanic motion, using both hands
and every nerve in my body,
I flip the big switch
off.

Off.
That quiet.
Loud stunning quiet.
Paralysis of storm quiet.

I walk away from the switch
terrified out of my mind,
also mindlessly happy while
the eye of the tempest passes over.

This time maybe there won't be cannons
and guns and flags waving,
nobody in the streets, fists raised,
shouting:
    No more!
Only tired lines of worried people
waiting at gas tanks, soup kitchens,
Red Cross supply vans, stores,

waiting with their worthless bills,
with the fresh memory of the way
           things should be
without a map for getting anywhere else.

    What a terrible day.

          Meanwhile,
those who saw the future,
who did not accept the lies,
who listened to science and reason
    and their unambiguous hearts,

who turned off their televisions just in time,
    shut the newspapers,
used them to start the first fires —

those people will already be entering
    their small fields, in their hands
        some kind of tool
without
a trace of unhappiness
        on their faces.

The sun will have leapt over the pines,
    the far ridge,
the windmill, the barn's cupola.

In that moment before the mist
begins to evaporate, when every leaf-blade
is bathed and fresh, silver-cast,

sun
poised

at the edges of fields
                    they will turn

to look back at their own tender footsteps
in the ephemeral dew.

Future-Seeking

i.

I am filling my hope chest.
In it I have
a rake, a hoe, an adze, a froe,
shovel, hammer, a curved knife,
a machete, an axe, a hatchet,
handsaw, drawing knife, scraper,
a screwdriver, pair of pliers, chisels,
wrenches, shears, a set of needles,
scissors, an awl, an anvil, a sledge,
clippers, a knife sharpener, file,
hole-diggers, a broom,
a pocketknife.
Can you think of anything
else I might need?

ii.

At our house
we have a machine
for
keeping milk cool
hearing news
writing letters
turning fruit to juice
answering our phone
toasting bread
mixing cakes
washing clothes
cutting firewood
splitting firewood
listening to music
recording ourselves
taking pictures
sewing
sawing
sealing
drilling holes
turning wood
sharpening pencils
tuning guitars
sweeping floors
heating water
warming the house
cooling the house
sucking moisture from air
brushing teeth
drying hair
popping popcorn.
I have taken more
than my fair share.

iii.

I will miss the old days
of driving for pleasure,
sweeping along the river road
or the coastal highway,
brilliant fall foliage
along Flathead Lake,
more dazzling
than the Emmys
or Disney World,
us kids on
the back of a pickup,
Mama and Daddy in the cab
their windows open
and open road
before us, or
late on a winter evening
snow piled
on fir boughs, a darkness
covering the absolute,
us safe in our autos
and warm, going home.

I will miss the pleasure
of effortless movement,
long fascination
with
speed.

Goodbye, beautiful ease.

I am relearning
the pleasures of these
slow
feet.

iv.

Everything I have learned
leads me to an age of bells,
timpani inside corollas

of bellflowers, gongs of trumpet
flowers, a thousand thousand
chimes of meadowbeauty

ringing in the fields.

V.

In the boardinghouse of hens
the Araucana has laid another green egg.
Strident and aloof, she is alert for army worms
parachuting from the trees.
She is Chilean, from the south of that country.
She is the most beautiful hen.
She rummages in the mineral soil,
far from the painted rooster.
Her fine, thick-shelled eggs
are disdainful gifts,
we her lucky patrons.

Remnant People in a Remnant Land

A barn longs for the trees it was,
        history
of forest, years circling in wood.
        A barn
never forgets. Its rafters remember
        sky.
What once held leaves
        and wind,
songs of vireos and thrushes,
        then
knew the shifting of
        horses,
knew the lowing of cows,
        is silent
in the evenings, after we have taken
        our bowls
to be washed and turned off the lights.
        No ewes
lick trough-oats, no streams of milk.
        Gone
the cock's crow, hens gabbling.
        Gone the sire.
               If
a barn has no animals, what gives it
        life?
A barn desires hay and the fragrance
        of hay.
A barn wishes for tools,
        a place
for every pitchfork. It desires carts,
        wheelbarrows,
bags of seed, buckets, moldboards,
        plows,

mowing machines, and
       whatever else
we've forgotten. More than
       anything,
a barn longs for barnsmen and barnswomen
       working
in the quiet
       while
wrens mistake beams for
       branches
as night comes on.

Justice

Let them have their oil.
Let them have their mosques and holy books,
the sun gleaming on the face of a woman
kneeling for the fifth time to pray.
Let her have the baby in her arms.
Let her bring from market the lentils, lamb,
bouquet of cilantro, cloves
that taste like the dusty rock of house
walls bordering the street.
Let her have the woven rug red and blue
beneath her real feet.
Let her have the pot, and the wooden ladle,
and the quiet ticking of a clock she no longer notices.
Let her have the common bird singing from the olive
and the sound of a door opening as it should.

And let me have my farm.
Let me have small clouds of breath as I rise
from patchwork quilts in the winter house.
Let me have a fallen maple for firewood
and the fire itself an eager bed of coals.
Let me have bowls of oatmeal and cups of tea
sweetened with tupelo honey, steaming
on the white enamel table.
Let me have my husband pulling on boots
to plant potatoes, while the moon
pauses in the sign for roots.
Let me have brown eggs still warm
from the hens, milk hot from the cow.
Let me have the common bird singing from the oak
and the sound of a door opening as it should.

Waiting in the Dark

Some nights when news is bad in the world
we go out and look at the sky,
which is dark even before the work day ends
save for pinpoints of stars and sometimes
an ivory disk sailing across it
over the shoulder of Wantastiquet.
The garden has disappeared under a trace of frost,
and Ezekiel Goodband's barn is filled
with heirloom apples. The yellow haze of maples
has faded, and the last of the leaves have fallen
like old newspaper and been swept up.

Come, darkness, with your longing.
Come with your rags and your death.
No one faults you the lies, the deceit.
You were meant for rest and sleep.

At solstice we will build a bonfire
on a hillside, a friend's field, beyond
greenhouse and pen, to watch the wine-moon
rise over the horizon like a chariot drawn
by dark horses. The moon will come close,
bright and orange as a winter squash, traveling
the long night. We will run up the hill to greet it.
The children will wave their little flags.
Remember how Mars one autumn
hovered as close to Earth as it had
in sixty thousand years, then drifted away?
These are the last days of the leaving.
We have entered the coming back.

Water

We drink it.
We rinse our hands in it.
We dip our faces in its coolness
and hold them there.
We swim in it in suits made especially for it,
and sometimes with all our clothes on
we jump into it.

Our bodies are mostly made of it, and we need it.
We get desperate for it, parched,
and when we are thus thirsty we go
to any lengths to find it.

We carry it with us in bottles
and jugs, in plastic bags.
We collect it in barrels,
pitchers and tanks.
We offer it to each other as gifts
when we visit each other's homes.
Under the hot sun we hold it
in cups and dippers
to each other's lips,
and we watch each other drink.
We offer it to our plants, to our crops,
to our trees, and to our animals,
and we watch them drink.

We gather food from it —
shrimp and crabs, cress and geese,
fish and turtles and potato root —
and we leave mounds
of shells and stems and bones alongside it.
We go to the edges of it,

and we shoot the animals that
come there, like us, to drink.
Sometimes we eat them,
and sometimes we simply throw
their limp bodies in.
Sometimes we eat part of them and
throw the rest in.

For hours we sit in vessels upon
it, hoping
to see strange creatures
that live in it, as we
cannot live—
whales, anhingas, seals —
and be seen by them.
Sometimes when we see these creatures,
we tremble in awe and disbelief,
and sometimes
we kill them.
We study their bodies
to see what we should know.

With powders and soaps and oils,
shampoos and conditioners,
we bathe in it.
We wash our clothes in it.
We wash our floors and our dishes and our fruit
before we eat, and our cars
and everything that needs to be washed
we wash in it.
We wash our children in it.

We urinate in it and defecate in it
and spit in it. We dump our waste
in it, motor oil and sewage and chemicals.
We dump our trash in it.

We throw the dead bodies of our enemies in it.

For everything we make, we use it.
We mix it with our paint.
We put it in our cakes and caulking and creosote.
We use it to wash the wood pulp that makes our paper,
and we add bleach to turn our paper white
and to whiten our sugar and our shirts and our socks.

Then we figure out complex ways to clean it.
We distill it and evaporate it
and diffuse it with ultraviolet light
and add chemicals to react
with the chemicals with which we have polluted it,
so we may use it over and over again.

We use it to run our turbines
and our locomotives and our cars and our steam
irons, and, like us, most of our machines
depend on it.
We use it to cool our engines
and nuclear rods, pipes and houses.

We cut the trees up to its edges —
cypress, tupelo and water hickory, slash
pine, live oak, and cabbage palm that love it, and

strip away the verdure — titi and fetterbush,
gallberry and cattails, needlerush and spartina —
that thrive along it and in it and also love it.

We banish the wild
sturgeon that grow strong in its currents,
wood ducks and spiny mussels, dragonflies
and banded watersnakes
that need it.

When it no longer contains shad,
cooter, alligator,
pitcher plant and iris, bladderwort,
we wonder what happened.
We hate it for not being what
we remember it to be.

We dam it and ditch it and build canals
for it to run through and
take great mountains of dirt
to cover the places where it is found.
We make new things in these places.
With our bulldozers we excavate
new courses and make it go
where we desire it to flow.
We force it to run in lines instead of curves.
We build levees and dikes to keep it out.
We build holding ponds.

We give it concrete banks
instead of sand ones,
instead of mud ones, clay ones,
jeweled rock ones.

We plow up to its edges and fill it
with sediment and turn it new colors
and change its habits and temperatures
and temperaments.

In our zeal to recreate the world
we annihilate bodies of it:
bogs and savannahs and sloughs,
domes where kingfishers fish,
ephemeral palaces of fairy shrimp,
vernal pools beside which flatwood
salamanders breed and tree frogs wait

on spring nights, calling
to the ones they love, "Come."
We destroy
creeks and mudflats and drains.

Sometimes we demolish
entire marshes, rivers, bays and lagoons.
Even oceans.

When it begins to get scarce around us,
in drouth, we irrigate with it.
We dip it out by hand or with great
helicopter buckets, suck it through hoses
to put out our fires.

In one of our greatest ironies
we have been known to cover it
with slicks of oil
and set fire to it.

We know it has many forms.
We know all its forms —
dew, rain, mist, fog,
drizzle,
ice, snow, sleet,
vapor, steam.
We are jealous of shapeshifting.

We go to great lengths
to build fleets that ride upon it
so that we may be with it but
not inside its mouth,
and we name these boats
after ourselves.

We race upon it.

We float our goods to and fro
upon it.
We look down into its depths and shudder.
Sometimes we strap bottles of air
on our backs
and we go down into it,
looking at what it has created,
which is mostly hidden
from us.
We look for things
we have lost in it.

We harness it,
for we are afraid of it.

It chokes us and fills
our lungs until we can no longer
breathe.
It sweeps over us in sudden tidal waves.
It surges up and laps us off our gondolas.
It turns into funnels and sucks us
off our yachts.

It turns to flood and takes away
everything we own.
We are nothing compared to its force.
Over millennia it wears even obsidian away.
It turns dead wood to grace.

And yet,
after a day in which we have used it
minute by minute
for our own will

we go down to it.
We take off our shoes and wade in it.

We cool our tired feet.
We take off all our clothes
and vault across its silvery surfaces,
like dolphins or whales,
and sometimes we simply rest,

floating
in it.

The first nine months of our lives
we live in it.
It is our beginning
as it is the beginning of everything.
It is elemental.
Thus we desire to return to it.
Thus we hold it sacred.
Thus we make it holy and bless it.
Thus we bless ourselves with it by sprinkling it on our heads
and on our holy things.
In the ultimate act of ablution
our holy men and women submerge us entirely in it.

We know the holiest among us have walked upon it.
We worship it.
We build shrines to it.
We hold festivals in honor of it
and in honor of the places where it is found.
We name things for those places —
towns and streets and cars,
businesses and each other.

We are most comfortable near it,
or beside it, or in it.
It is the greatest gift we have.
It is boundless.
It belongs to us.

It can not be destroyed.
Yet we destroy it.

We stand in awe before it.
We stand in fear before it.
We stand in need before it.

For years of our lives
we simply stand before it.

Sleeping in the Forest

Flowering wiregrass brushes against a brass bed
in the longleaf pines.

Feathers in the pillows go to seed
below a canopy of green.

Woodpecker chicks nestle in down
within the brown columns of trees.

Limb against limb, sometimes
with murmurs, the pines touch each other.

The forest is a place no one will come.
How the bed got there does not matter.

The sleepers are tired from all
they fought to keep — and lost.

This is not the time to think what the children's
lives will be like, or what will happen

to the town with a new mall.
This is the place sleep is possible.

Let kestrels hunt evening.
Let bluebirds fetch dreams.

When a coyote happens upon the sleepers,
it stands a long time watching.

Pray for Blue Jay Memory to Fail

Pray the blue jays have scoured oak,
pinyon, beech, hickory

and buried their caches
wildly scattered about.

Pray the barren winter scrambles
landmarks inside their delicate,

blue-filled skulls, and
for their picketing and squawking

to occupy them to distraction.
Pray the nuts and seeds

remain faithful, through long cold,
to the anticipation of spring

and for sun-warmth to reach acorns
before hunger.

Then a new forest already pushes
upward through the grass.

Fire-Wings II

Where does its fire go
when a monarch dies?
Does it vanish
in smoke or turn
suddenly to rain?
Does it lie dead
against a mountainside
transforming placidly
to dirt, which
will harbor in its richness
millions of small burning ships
sailing a deep-green forest,
never to be seen? Or
does the fire seep into the ground,
running in rivulets
toward the blazing core
of the earth,
one day to return,
a volcano
spewing wings?

Flight of the Queen

What are these,
humming and fighting in a thick hive

near a rack of washed-up spartina
in and out of sunshine?

They land on sea oxeye flowers.
Chasing and clasping, they roil to the ground.

Certainly they are wasps, yes, with three parts to the body,
smoked-glass eyes

huge and wise to ferocity,
faces of topaz gods.

Yet they are like no wasps I've seen — bigger,
warriors whose wars swept them

sometime in the night
to this barrier island

where the tide came in and went out
while we slept.

A painted bunting flies from live oak to cedar
above their distress.

What are they searching for
among last year's dry reeds, hovering

low, and why, when they meet,
do they seethe and curse

in high pitches, battle-locked,
jousting with their six legs, stingers out?

Not long ago someone asked me:
What is it you fundamentally want,

and what, to have it, will you give?
(A question I could not answer.)

It is mid-morning when finally
I see the queen wasp. She is even bigger

and not so dark, tangled in grass.
Like electrons males circle and zing around her.

Even as one mates, others bombard
to tear him loose and take his place.

They are answering
the only question they were given.

Their path to the queen
is not mythological, only brutal.

I am not saying I want my life fixed, calendar
on a wall. Nor that I want more.

I am saying I am still ignorant,
blind with questions.

Wishing to Be Dove-like

You are sitting in the dark
trying to figure out for yourself
what your life is made of.
I see you there, expectant,
eager for the information that will
save you, your children, all of us.
You are waiting
to see if I will deliver it, if I
have been praying and thinking,
meditating and dreaming
deep enough to deliver it.
Oh my sweetness,
my dear, if only I had
one long wing white and strong
I would use it
to sweep you up, I would say
nothing, offer nothing
but that soft wing,
sliding toward you,
gentle and permanent,
and I would touch you with it,
wrap you with that long beam
of perfect light.
You would be comforted, your life
different, touched
with something magnificent,
undeniable, and true.
But, my friend, you can see
that I have not found
that long wing constructed of light.
I am still looking.

Pressing Cider at Deer Ridge Farm

Our hands reach through dry weed-stalks
to gather Baldwins and Winesaps
fallen into brown rucksacks of leaves,

two, three at a time. They fill a crate,
apples thunking. Our hands carry
bins through the overgrown orchard

down to the cider press beside the shed.
Our hands rinse the apples, toss them
one by one into a hand-made mill.

Our hands funnel the juice, collect pulp.
Our hands empty and wring and pour.
They fasten and tighten and twist.

Our hands cup the solemn red.
Steady the wooden lid of the chute.
Love the astonishment of cold water.

Our hands praise. Our hands transform.
Our hands take a charity of apples
and bring forth benediction.

600 Gallons of Fresh Milk

A month after Hurricane Katrina
tore through New Orleans,
two days after the most intense
earthquake ever hit Pakistan,
the day after Vermont flooded,
after we worked hours
sweeping and sopping water
from our own ruined basement
and had slept poorly,
briefly, that morning —
although roads were bad, bridges
washed out, with the sky
still drizzling and more rain
predicted to fall —
I went for milk.
Fields were thick
with vines, farmstands
ripe with pumpkins.
At the dairy barn, swallows
flew from the hayloft
into first sun.
A few cows had not been taken
from their stanchions,
and bags full,
watched me arrive with my jars,
into the milkhouse, through the door
with the missing screen.
I lifted the lid of the tank.
It was full,
almost overflowing,
a white nourishment,
sweet-smelling, entirely
beyond tragedy,

and floating with cream.
I stared and stared.
Oh, the relief of it.
The beauty.
Think what our lives will look like
when we get them back.

Grace Will Lead Us Home

I'll pay more attention.
I'll write down glimpses
of coyote, emerald insect.
Every January a bird list:
Carolina wren, chickadee,
beautiful arrow of cardinal
glanced at the apple tree.
I'll build a blind to watch
wild turkeys, deer
come to salt. Mapping,
I'll leave places unnamed.
Memorize binomials
of the grasses.
Buy a rain gauge,
sling a hammock,
and read more, maybe
kill a deer come fall.
I'll plant rosemary, moonflower,
go outside summer nights
when heat lightning rips
pink-orange clouds. I'll plot
Jupiter's moons before bed.
First frost. Last.
Sandhill cranes overhead.
The mating of anoles.
I'll walk deliberately, quietly,
discover more of what
rises and falls.
Length of night, winter,
how long a year.
What better to be
than a particular
body of knowledge,

leaping
the branch, courting
pine and field, listening
to this hallowed ground.

Courage

Intrepid by instinct, a loon
floats in the torn silk of summer morning,
placid through mist rising like white fire, a burning water
that holds the new green of hemlock in its light.
Everywhere the blue of lupine rages.

All afternoon, into the long spill of Yaak twilight
until there is hardly a seam to the day, the single loon
serenely dives, again and again, into shivering water,
plying a clouded bottom.
Sometimes all day, days, rain falls. Night comes.

Once I came upon a softshell turtle
newly killed. All night it sat in my refrigerator.
Next morning, dressing it, I found the heart still pumping,
robust, though every other part lay stiff. Eerily the heart
throbbed, majestic and crazed in my hand.

The turtle did not die of failure of the heart,
mad desire of one radiant ember within us all.
Hours afterward in a bowl of water it beat.
Hours afterward it
pounded.

Let it not be said that in passing through this world
you turned your face and left its wounds unattended.
Instead, let it be said that when your friends
cut open your chest to partake of its courage,
a loon was calling.

— Notes —

"Courage" contains a line that was spoken by Barry Lopez at The Orion Society's June 1999 conference, "Fire and Grit: Working for Nature in Community" — "Let it not be said that in passing through this world you turned your head and left its wounds unattended." My poem is written out of love for the Yaak Valley of Montana, with hope that its last unroaded and untrammeled places will be legally protected as wilderness by a visionary Congress.

The title "remnant people in a remnant land" comes from Wendell Berry in *The Long-Legged House* (Shoemaker and Hoard, 2004). Berry's sentence is "We are a remnant people in a remnant country."

"Water" was written in the style of a long prose poem by Pattiann Rogers about the human relationship with animals, called "Animals and People: The Human Heart in Conflict with Itself." Rogers's poem was published in the Winter 1997 issue of *Orion* Magazine and can be found online at http://arts.envirolink/literary_arts. The poem "Water" looks at the human relationship with water and an inherent conflict found there. It was performed as spoken word by Dana Skelton for a trapeze dance show, "Water Body," April 18-20 and 25-27, 2008 at Canopy Studio, Athens, Georgia, directed by aerialist Susan Murphy.

— Acknowledgments —

Some of these poems appeared in a limited-edition chapbook, *Naming the Unseen*, published in 1996 by the University of Montana, the prize of the Merriam-Frontier Award. I thank Tony Crunk, Mark Levine, and Greg Pape for selecting the manuscript, as well as Roger Dunsmore and Patricia Traxler for their thorough and generous critiques.

I thank the journals and books in which the following poems, in one form or another, first appeared:

A Summer's Reading: "Cardinal Flowers" and "Bird-Banding with the Biologists"

Alaska Quarterly Review: "Rescue"

Asheville Poetry Review: "Creation Story" and "On the Beach One Summer Night After Hearing the Algae Is On"

Blackbird on My Shoulder: Stories and Other Truths from the South (edited by Lisa Alembik): "Land of Milk and Honey"

Elemental South: An Anthology of Southern Nature Writing (edited by Dorinda Dallmeyer): "Courage," "Edge of the World," "Fire-Wings I," "Fire-Wings II," and "Riding Bareback through the Universe"

Georgia Review: "Tympanum"

Heartstone: "Water"

Pegasus: "Justice"

Talking River Review: "Orchard"

*We All Live Downstream: Writings about Mountaintop Removal (*edited by Jason Howard), part of "Revolution"

ISLE (Interdisciplinary Studies in Literature and Environment):"Bird-Banding with the Biologists," "Bone Deposit," and "Tympanum"

— Gratitude —

I am grateful for my teachers, who did the best they could with my stubbornness and limitations, including Rick Bass, Wendell Berry, Lucille Clifton, Jack Gilbert, Jane Hirshfield, David Kirby, Pattiann Rogers, and Patricia Traxler.

Some gracious and brilliant friends have read and critiqued this manuscript, and their suggestions and insights have been invaluable. For this I thank Emilie Buchwald, Daniel Corrie, Roger Dunsmore, Ann Fisher-Wirth, and Patricia Traxler.

I thank all poets, writers, and editors whose friendship, camaraderie, and work sustain me, and especially I thank Rick Bass, Wendell and Tanya Berry, Emerson Blake, Franklin Burroughs, Kathryn Byer, Susan Cerulean, Daniel Corrie, Thomas Rain Crowe, Dorinda Dallmeyer, Jan DeBlieu, Ann Fisher-Wirth, John Lane, Bill McKibben, Kathleen Dean Moore, Roger Pinckney, Mark Powell, Able Rae, Jennifer Sahn, Betsy Teter, and Jim Wohlpart. I honor the memory of my dear friend Milton N. Hopkins, inspiration for a number of these poems.

The debt I owe Charlie Hughes of Wind Publications, a true man of letters, is not quantifiable. When I had been swimming for a long time at sea, and was tired, with no land in sight, a boat appeared and he was in it. My gratitude for his willingness to bet a chunk of his time and his wallet on this book, and his faith in it, is bottomless.

A better literary agent than Sam Stoloff could not be found.

I want to acknowledge how honored I am to have on the cover of this book a painting ("Piedmont Savanna") by renowned landscape painter, and my friend, Philp Juras of Athens, Georgia. Philip is painting large landscapes of the Southern frontier in the tradition of the Hudson School, in his words, "to complete the picture begun by the 19th century American landscape movement — a movement instrumental in forming our national environmental ethic, but which started too late and too far north and west to include the southern wilderness." At last the South has been given a painter of awesome vision and breathtaking talent. Philip's work can be viewed at www.philipjuras.com.

Eleonora Alcalde Machado designed the cover. I am in awe of her creativity.

My father, Franklin Ray, told me when I was a child that saints and poets inherit the earth and I determined then to be one or the other. I thank him. I thank my mother, Lee Ada Branch Ray, for her love. Thanks to my extended family, Ian Amsler, Kay Amsler, Tom Amsler, Joette Mendez, Cherie Montanez, Dell Ray, Rita Carter Ray, and Carlin Joshua Ray, as well as Julian and Nya Bimini Mendez.

Without my wider family of friends, where would I be? Please know my deepest gratitude.

My son, Silas Ray-Burns, himself a poet, has shown me the vastness and fierceness of love. He also gave me great advice on the contents of this collection.

My husband, Raven Waters, is my constant and loving companion, wind and fire, moon and rain.

Thank you all.

— The Author —

Janisse Ray lives in the coastal plains of southeast Georgia, where she farms, studies nature, and writes. She is the author of three books of literary nonfiction, *Ecology of a Cracker Childhood, Wild Card Quilt: Taking a Chance on Home,* and *Pinhook: Finding Wholeness in a Fragmented Land.* She holds an MFA from the University of Montana, and in 2007 was awarded an honorary doctorate from Unity College in Maine. She is on the faculty of Chatham University's low-residency MFA program and is a Woodrow Wilson Visiting Fellow. She and her husband, Raven Waters, have three grown children and two grandchildren.

CPSIA information can be obtained at www.ICGtesting.com

262241BV00001B/28/P